D1501978

ONTARIO

ONTARIO

CHARTWELL
BOOKS, INC.

This edition published in 2008 by

CHARTWELL BOOKS, INC.
A Division of
BOOK SALES, INC.
114 Northfield Avenue
Edison, New Jersey 08837

ISBN13: 978-0-7858-2459-6
ISBN10: 0-7858-2459-6

© 2008 Compendium Publishing,
43 Frith Street, London, Soho, W1D 4SA, United Kingdom

Cataloging-in-Publication data is available from the
Library of Congress

Printed and bound in China

Design: Mark Tennent/Compendium Design

PAGE 2: Parliament Buildings and the Rideau Canal in Ottawa
(iStockphoto 2191608 Ronnie Comeau).

RIGHT: The Horseshoe Falls at night *(Fotolia 4825760 Kamwise).*

Contents

Introduction

The Toronto skyline at dusk
(iStockphoto 4096879 Eberth Rodriguez).

Introduction

The origins of the name Ontario is unclear; it possibly derives from the Huron word meaning "great lake" or from the word *skanadario* or "beautiful water". As a province, located in central Canada, Ontario is bordered by Manitoba to the west and Quebec to the east. Its borders with the United States (comprising Michigan, Minnesota and New York) are mainly natural along the stunning backdrops of the Lake of the Woods and the four Great Lakes—Superior, Huron, Erie and Ontario—after which this enchanting province is named. Ontario also borders the St Lawrence River where it runs through Cornwall, an ancient town lying to the east of Ottawa, close to the boundary with Quebec.

While Quebec has the greatest land mass in Canada, Ontario has the largest population of more than 12,850,630, which accounts for nearly thirty-nine percent of the country's total population. Although Ottawa (Canada's capital city) is found here, the largest city in the province—which is also Ontario's capital—is Toronto. Ontario has a historic past and was one of the four original provinces (alongside Quebec, Nova Scotia and New Brunswick) established in Canada on July 1, 1867, when the country was formed by the British North America Act.

There are four geographical regions here: the Canadian Shield; the Hudson Bay Lowlands; the Great Lakes and St Lawrence Valley; and, Southern Ontario. This latter land mass is further divided into Central, Eastern, Golden Horseshoe and South-Western Ontario which was formerly referred to as Western Ontario. The region comprising the Great Lakes and the St Lawrence Valley to the south of the province has a temperate climate, and much of the area here is dominated by fertile lands and, unsurprisingly, agriculture. Located in the extreme north and northeast is the vastly unpopulated Hudson Bay Lowlands with its swamps and sparse forests while the northwest and central parts of the province belong to the Canadian Shield. This region is also mainly unpopulated due to its unfertile land, however, the area is rich in minerals and beautiful landscapes with its lakes and rivers.

Many people living in Ontario today are descendants of British and other Europeans who settled in the province while those with French ancestry make up around eleven percent of the population. Over the past two centuries, immigrants have continued to flock to the area, although more recent arrivals have included peoples of other countries and cultures including those from Asia (such as China, Sri Lanka, India, Pakistan and Bangladesh) as well as those from the Caribbean and South America. However, immigration does not stop there and many smaller groups have settled including people from Bosnia, Russia, Iran and parts of Africa. It was all very different though in the early days of the province's history.

Originally, the land was populated by two peoples: the Algonquians (made up of Ojibwa, Algonquin and Cree tribes) and the Iroquoians, who consisted of Iroquois and Huron tribes. The French and British arrived around the same time in the early seventeenth century; French explorer Étienne Brûlé toured part of

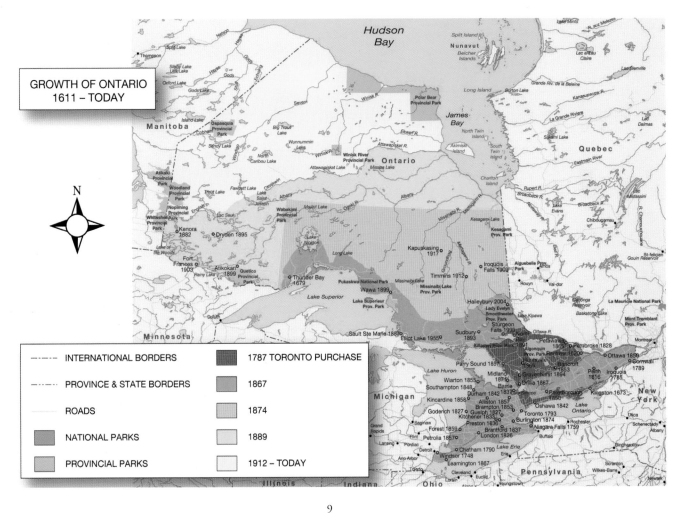

GROWTH OF ONTARIO
1611 – TODAY

Legend:
- INTERNATIONAL BORDERS
- PROVINCE & STATE BORDERS
- ROADS
- NATIONAL PARKS
- PROVINCIAL PARKS
- 1787 TORONTO PURCHASE
- 1867
- 1874
- 1889
- 1912 – TODAY

the area between 1608 and 1612, while Henry Hudson, from England, landed in what became known as Hudson Bay in 1611. By 1615, French missionaries were beginning to establish themselves along the Great Lakes, although progress was somewhat hampered by the Iroquois tribes who became allies of the British. This prompted a struggle for domination in Ontario and the Seven Years War came to an end with the Treaty of Paris in 1763. The following century saw the province come under attack from American troops in the 1812 War. The British successfully defeated the neighboring invaders, despite the American's occupation of York (having won the Battle of York) the following year. This town was later renamed Toronto. The American troops were soon forced out following widespread looting and a period of stability would see the arrival of many immigrants from across the Atlantic.

Like many parts of North America, Ontario benefited from an economic boom during the 1850s through the advent of the railroads which facilitated expansion and development. However, the American Civil War (1861–65), coupled with continuing struggles between the French and British, led to political conferences the following decade which implemented change with the instigation of the British North America Act in 1867.

The province, today, is a huge manufacturing area and more than fifty-two percent of the country's total output originates in Ontario. Following the establishment of Canada as a country and Ontario as a

LEFT: This engraving depicts the junction of the St Lawrence and Ottawa Rivers in the early 1800s with two large rafts, each steered by six people, afloat in the central channel *(Getty Images 2847768 Hulton Archive/Getty Images)*

province, minerals became an important resource. Mining was accelerated during the late nineteenth century and Ontario's many water resources were utilized to full effect by creating hydro-electric power. Despite the increase in mining and agricultural activities, power was still bitterly sought, and in the early 1900s, there was a move to limit the availability of French-language schooling. Prohibition was introduced in 1916 (although distilling and maintaining a personal supply of alcohol was permitted, as was distillation and export for sale). The end of the Second World War would see dramatic prosperity and development in Ontario, when the advent of the nationalist movement in Quebec forced many English-speaking people out of the province along with profitable businesses, who in turn changed the fortunes of Ontario and helped to establish one of the most enterprising and economically sound provincial areas in Canada.

Covering an area of 415,598 square miles (1,076,395 square kilometers), Ontario is rich in its diverse landscapes, flora and fauna. Around sixty-six percent of Ontario's landmass is forested, approximately ninety percent of which is owned by the province. These forests are comprised of Jack Pine, Red Pine, White Pine, Black Spruce, White Spruce, Oak, Hard Maple, Cedar, Poplar and Larch trees to name but a few. About a third of the forests are classified as production forests, meaning that they are cultivated and maintained for timber production. These massive areas which predominantly characterize the province are roughly equal to the landmass of Germany, Switzerland, Italy and the Netherlands combined. The forests are home to a myriad of plants and animals including more than 3,200 plant species, 160 types of fish, 80

species of amphibians and reptiles as well as 400 species of birds and around 85 specials of mammals. The Great Lakes, and their connecting channels, form the largest freshwater system on earth. Covering more than 94,000 square miles (243,458 square kilometers), Superior, Michigan, Huron, Erie and Ontario, hold around one-fifth of the world's fresh water supply. These freshwater seas greatly affect the way of life in Ontario from weather and climate to wildlife and habitat and, today, are recognized as a fragile part of the national ecosystem which needs careful management to ensure conservation. From its landscapes, industry, wildlife to its towns and cities, Ontario is rich in history, diverse in its peoples and has much to offer anyone living in, or visiting this magical province.

LEFT AND ABOVE: Ontario boasts numerous habitats, from the hustle and bustle of cities like Toronto *(Fotolia 4754889 Gary Blakeley)* to the rugged peacefulness of the wild *(Fotolia 6140412 Elena Elisseeva)*.

ABOVE: Tourists board their bus in the city of Niagara Falls in preparation for their trip to see the wonders of nature *(iStockphoto 4330846 Tony Tremblay)*.

RIGHT: The building that houses the Supreme Court of Canada in Ottawa was designed by Ernest Cormier and is situated just west of the Parliament Buildings on a bluff high above the Ottawa River *(Fotolia 514729 Howard Sandler)*.

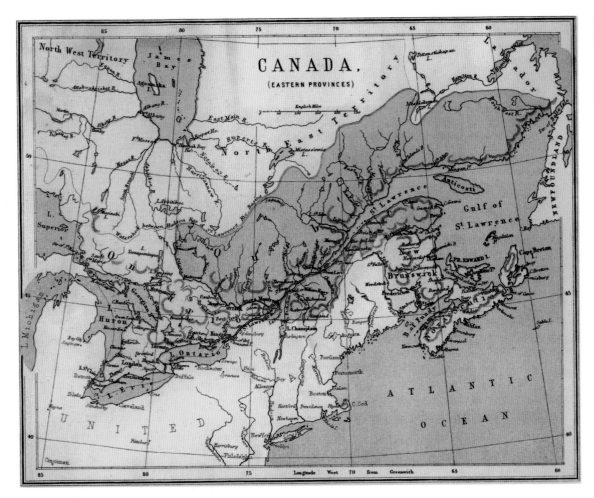

A map of the eastern provinces of Canada during the late-nineteenth century

LEFT: Fishermen and boats at the quayside in Toronto around 1841 *(Getty Images 3071080 Hulton Archive/Getty Images).*

ABOVE: The historic Old City Hall in downtown Toronto *(Fotolia 5890236 Mary Lane).*

RIGHT: Built at a cost of more than $3,500,000 between 1911 and 1914, Toronto's Casa Loma is a cacophony of stately towers, soaring battlements, secret passageways and sweeping terraces *(Fotolia 4228799 MichaelM)*.

FAR RIGHT: The rocky landscape of the Canadian Shield *(iStockphoto 5072996 Sebastian Santa)*.

OVERLEAF: A panorama of Crystal Beach on the shores of Lake Erie *(LoC pan 6a22587)*.

LEFT: Granite cliffs and White pines typify the landscape in Killarney Provincial Park, one of Ontario's most popular wilderness destinations. With its sapphire blue lakes and white quartzite ridges, it is considered the crown jewel of the Ontario Park system *(Getty Images 79382865 Glenn Bartley).*

FAR LEFT: The natural beauty of the Algonquin Provincial Park is plain to see *(Fotolia 1223440 Elena Elisseeva)*.

LEFT: Skiing has become a popular and lucrative pastime during the Canadian winter *(Fotolia 459883 Elena Elisseeva)*.

LEFT: The picturesque Toronto waterfront (*Fotolia 1158274 Elena Elisseeva*).

ABOVE: The *Maid of the Mist* takes tourists into the spray at Horseshoe Falls (*iStockphoto 3783909 Howard Sandler*).

OVERLEAF: The Canadian Tulip Festival claims to be the largest of its kind in the world, with more than 500,000 visitors each year. This major cultural event is held in Ottawa and Gatineau in May (*Getty Images 79382725 Don Johnston*).

ABOVE: A fiery sunset lights up the sky over Georgian Bay *(Getty Images 51452030 National Geographic/Getty Images)*.

RIGHT: A wind turbine feeds renewable electricity into the Ontario grid at the CNE grounds in Toronto *(Corbis 42-17945542 J P Moczulski /Reuters/Corbis)*.

FAR LEFT: A memorial flame burns on Parliament Hill in Ottawa *(iStockphoto 3625288 calvio).*

LEFT: Fireworks light up the Toronto waterfront *(Fotolia 3395899 Elena Elisseeva).*

LEFT: Ice skaters glide along Ottawa's Rideau Canal
(iStockphoto 2852167 James G Charron).

ABOVE: A breach loaded cannon with riffled barrel at Fort Henry, Kingston
(iStockphoto 3980949 Ian Breckenridge).

Indigenous peoples and discovery (–1700)

One of the primary aims of the Algonquin Provincial Park is to provide visitors with an idea of how Ontario looked before it was colonized *(Fotolia 3889076 Kim D French)*.

Indigenous peoples and discovery (–1700)

The earliest, undisputed, evidence of human settlement in Canada is found on the Haida Gwaii (Queen Charlotte Islands) in British Columbia. Nanu, is an archaeological site dated from around 12,000 years ago where Ice Age hunters and gatherers left fluted stone tools and the remains of large butchered mammals. This site is recognized as that of the longest continuous human occupation in Canada. From here, and sites like it, came the native peoples that eventually settled in what was to become Ontario. The Algonquian and Iroquoian tribes—two unrelated families—were the first known settlers in the region. The Algonquian groups occupied much of the land around Lake Superior, north of Lake Huron to the Ottawa Valley, while the Iroquoians settled mainly in southern Ontario and the St Lawrence Valley as far east as the area which would become the city of Quebec.

The first foreign visitors to Ontario were Norse – who made a number of sporadic visits to the eastern shores of Canada between the tenth and fourteenth centuries to primarily exchange goods. But, it was the Europeans who first "discovered" the area and it was these relative newcomers, including French and British explorers in the sixteenth and seventeenth centuries, who were keen to declare these native peoples' lands their own. One of the first to arrive was Frenchman Jacques Cartier (1491–1557), who described and mapped the shores of the St Lawrence River and the Gulf of St Lawrence on a

ABOVE: It is easy to visualize early explorers meeting with natives beside the clear waters of Georgian Bay on the Bruce Peninsula *(Fotolia 5987413 Elena Elisseeva).*

RIGHT: A map of the country of the Five Nations or Iroquois—now belonging to the province of New York, as well as part of Canada and Lakes Huron, Michigan, Superior, Erie and Ontario—circa 1650. The Five Nations was a league of Native Americans founded in the sixteenth century *(Getty Images 51246094 MPI/Getty Images)*

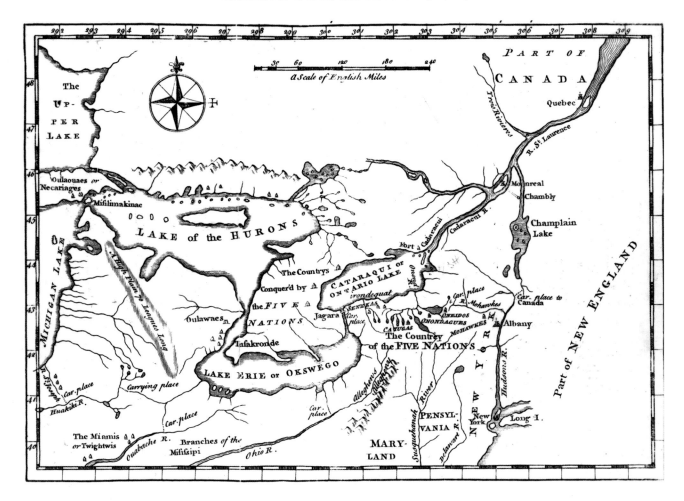

ABOVE: A depiction of traders near the Cat Falls on the Ottawa River. These falls are no longer as spectacular as they are now regulated by a hydro-electric dam (LoC cph 3g03303).

Étienne Brûlé (1592–1633) came to "New France" in 1608 and took to the way of life of the "First Nations", the Canadian name for the aboriginal peoples. He began living with the Huron people in 1610 and became a scout for Samuel de Champlain (1580–1635) where he explored much of what is now Ontario. Brûlé was so excited by his new home and the native people who treated him like their own that he left de Champlain's camp to take up permanent residence with the natives where he discovered the pathway to the Humbers, historically a fishing area for the First Nations. Meanwhile, de Champlain, who founded the city of Quebec in 1608, began trying to build relationships with Huron and Algonquian. Forming alliances with the tribes, de Champlain agreed to fight against the Iroquoians. An ensuing battle, which saw the Iroquoians turn from de Champlain and flee, would set the tone between the French and the native tribe for the next 100 years.

This defeat of the Iroquois at Ticonderoga saw the tribes ally with the Dutch who were willing to trade firearms in return for fur. However, by 1640, the beaver—the main supply of fur—was suffering a depletion of its natural habitat and a subsequent decrease in populations which, coupled with loss of human life through epidemics, reduced tribe numbers and therefore their dominance in the region dramatically.

land that he named Canada in 1534. Having been sent by King Francis I of France, Cartier was convinced on his arrival in Ontario that he had discovered the wealthy continent of Asia. He and his men traded knives and iron in exchange for furs with the native peoples and the Huron became the first large-scale to the fur trade.

RIGHT: Traveling by water was the quickest method of crossing the country (LoC cph 3b50174).

The Niagara Escarpment at Halfway Log Dump along Bruce Trail on the Bruce Penninsula National Park, near Tobermory. The Escarpment has been designated a World Biosphere Reserve by UNESCO, making it one of 12 in Canada. Development and land use adjacent to the escarpment is regulated and the biosphere protected by the Niagara Escarpment Commission, an agency of the Ontario government *(Getty Images 79382852 Henry Georgi)*.

ABOVE: Several tepees at a camp by Stony Lake (LoC cph 3a48512).

RIGHT: A stunning view of Niagara Falls, frozen during the harsh Canadian winter (Fotolia 3970245 Trent).

The Wye Marsh is still as spectacular as it was hundreds of years ago but is now designated as an Important Bird Area and home to an amazing diversity of bird species (*Fotolia 4049080 Focused*).

Weathered rocks and lichens on a
small island in the Fox Island group,
Georgian Bay
(*Getty Images 79382730 Don Johnston*).

The magnificent Silver Peak from
Granite Ridge viewpoint as summer
turns to fall in the Killarney
Provincial Park
(Getty Images 79382722 Don Johnston).

LEFT: The city of Kingston was first established in 1673 as Fort Cataraqui and was later renamed Fort Frontenac *(iStockphoto 4379294 Les Palenik).*

ABOVE: Of course, the vast majority of the early structures built in Canada have not withstood the ravages of time. This wooden church in Wicklow survived until 1986 before being destroyed by fire *(Corbis MF002528 Michael Freeman/Corbis).*

Kincardine Lighthouse at sunset on
Lake Huron
(Getty Images 73777984 Ethan Meleg).

FAR LEFT: A log cabin, typical of the more rural areas of Ontario (*Fotolia 1993124 Johan Kneslen*).

LEFT: A passenger steamship on Lake Muskoka, located between Port Carling and Gravenhurst (*iStockphoto 4327589 Les Palenik*).

A fight for dominance (1700–63)

An aerial view of Niagara Falls
(Fotolia 3804582 Howard Sandler).

A fight for dominance (1700–63)

During the latter part of the seventeenth century, Iroquoian power continued to wane and the Ojibwa and Algonquin tribes began to expand further into southern Ontario. (Descendants of these native peoples still occupy reserves in the region today.) In 1722, the former five nations became six when the Iroquois accepted the Tuscarora tribe, who had fled north from the Carolinas. Most Algonquians, however, were in league with the French and continued to supply them with furs in exchange for European commodities. But, apart from a group of Mohawk (who had settled near Montreal), the majority of Iroquois were allied to the British.

The continued struggles between the French and British for dominance in Ontario, as well as the rest of Canada, were about to get a decidedly worse with the advent of the Seven Years War. Britain, Prussia and Hanover embarked on the world's first global hostilities when they declared war on France, Austria, Sweden, Saxony, Russia (and eventually Spain) in 1756. Britain concentrated its efforts—and initiated hostilities in 1754—on the French navy and merchant fleet in a bid to seize its main commercial rival's colonies. It left Prussian and German mercenaries fighting the war back in Europe. For its part, France was unable to defend itself overseas (including in Canada) although the British forces were particularly unsuccessful on land. As the British army advanced on Lake Champlain, it was stopped by French forces near Lake George

in New York State in the US. But, in April 1756, with the arrival of more French troops, led by new commander the Marquis de Montcalm, Britain had had enough and declared war on their

ABOVE: A west view of Oswego and Fort Ontario with General Amherst's camp at Lake Ontario in 1760 (LoC cph 3a49137).

RIGHT: Pontiac (circa 1720–69), chief of the Ottawa tribe and leader of a federation of Native Americans against the settlers, smokes the peace pipe at a meeting with Major Rogers and his troops (Getty Images 2667134 MPI/Getty Images)

adversaries in May that same year. The tide turned on the French in 1758 and on Lake Ontario, at Fort Frontenac, the ensuing battle saw the fort destroyed (along with a great many supplies meant for French western posts) while Louisbourg and Guadeloupe were also taken by the British. The decimation of this key French foothold saw the Indian allies of the French agree separate treaties with the British, which in turn, forced other forts to be abandoned. In 1759, the British were well advanced into Ontario and were fast approaching Quebec. Following the Battle of the Plains of Abraham, outside Quebec, the French were once again defeated.

The end of the Seven Years War, or the French and Indian War, as it was also called, came with the Treaty of Paris which was signed on February 10, 1763. The treaty was to mark the beginning of an extensive period of British dominance in the province of Ontario when the French, who preferred to maintain control in Guadeloupe, gave up their rights to New France and all their territories east of the Mississippi River.

However, the odds had clearly been against France from the beginning. The superior British navy had been able to stop many French vessels from even reaching New France throughout the duration of the war. The French had an army of 5,000 soldiers in New France, while the British colonies had military might with troops numbering at least 23,000.

RIGHT: Boreal forest and driftwood along the shoreline at North Beach in Pukaskwa. Pukaskwa National Park is located south of the town of Marathon in the Thunder Bay District (*Getty Images 73777947 Ron Erwin*).

ABOVE: Agriculture has played a huge role in the prosperity of Ontario *(Fotolia 5923124 Elena Elisseeva).*

RIGHT: The Scarborough Bluffs are an escarpment along the shoreline of Lake Ontario that indicate the old shoreline of Lake Iroquois, formed after the last ice age *(iStockphoto 4879186 Arpad Benedek).*

RIGHT: Re-enactments of famous battles are popular with both the participants and onlookers
(iStockphoto 2897981 Chris McCooey).

FAR RIGHT: In 1793, Lieutenant Governor John Graves Simcoe authorized a garrison on the present site of Fort York, just west of the mouth of Garrison Creek on the north eastern shore of Lake Ontario. Most of the Fort was demolished in the Battle of York in 1813 and the buildings visible now were largely built by Royal Engineers immediately after. They are among the oldest buildings in Toronto today
(Corbis DH011606 Dave G Houser/Corbis).

FAR LEFT: Oxtongue River in the Algonquin Park *(iStockphoto 4519376 Grzegorz Malec).*

LEFT: Lion's Head lighthouse at dusk on the Bruce Peninsula *(Getty Images 200492273-001 Frank Krahmer).*

ABOVE: A panorama of Georgian Bay, part of Lake Huron. The Bay is about 320 kilometers long by 80 kilometers wide and covers over 15,000 square kilometers, making it almost as large as Lake Ontario (*Fotolia 5526242 Paddler*).

LEFT: The Ottawa River passes through the capital
(Corbis U1592330 Bettmann/Corbis).

OVERLEAF: The sun reflects on the surface of Eva Lake
(Getty Images 77163554 Paul Damien).

Life after the Seven Years War (1763–1900)

An industrial area of Hamilton in 1906
(LoC pan 6a23357).

Life after the Seven Years War (1763–1900)

New France was annexed to Quebec following the Treaty of Paris (1763), and Britain granted loyalists—leaving the United States as a result of the American War of Independence (1775–83)—200 acres which substantially increased the population in Ontario (and Canada elsewhere) west of the St Lawrence and Ottawa Rivers which was recognized in the Constitutional Act of 1791. However, during the war of 1812, American troops invaded what had become Upper Canada (southwest of the St Lawrence/Ottawa River confluence) and gained control of Lake Erie and Lake Ontario. But, the British, supported by Canadian militia and First Nation fighters, pushed the US armed forces back although they did take the town of York in 1813. Burning down the Parliamentary buildings—in the town that would later be renamed Toronto—the Americans were eventually forced out by the allies after heavy looting.

Although relative stability in Ontario was restored following the 1812 war, immigrants from the United States were few and far between. Many of the new arrivals were predominantly from England, Ireland, Scotland and Wales where immigration was deliberately encouraged by colonial leaders. But, despite the offers of free land (or affordable plots), life for the immigrants was particularly harsh. The climate was difficult for many and those with the resources to leave often moved south or returned home. However, Ontario's population increased dramatically in the first half of the 1800s in a way that it didn't before and hasn't since. This increase in population—combined with new roads, canal projects amongst other initiatives—helped to develop trade routes, particularly into the United States, which in turn brought about an upturn in long-term relationships. The array of waterways in Ontario also helped greatly in development. The numerous rivers and other waterways enabled faster travel and greater transportation as well as seeing the establishment of water power used in industry. Businesses began to grow and blossom while developed transportation networks aided an economic boom and growth in communications.

But, still there was unrest. Many in the colony were opposed to the aristocratic leadership which they endured that prohibited the establishment of elected bodies capable of effecting change. This led to resentment which gave rise to republican ideals and brought about early Canadian nationalism. A rebellion in Lower Canada was instigated by Louis-Joseph Papineau (1786–1871) while a similar rebellion was led in Upper Canada by William Lyon Mackenzie (1795–1861) who launched a series of bitter attacks on the British

RIGHT: This engraving depicts a view of the St Lawrence River in the early 1800s with several canoes in the distance (*Getty Images 2847806 Hulton Archive/Getty Images*).

provincial government through his newspaper, *Colonial Advocate*, in 1837. Despite being expelled from Upper Canada's elective legislative assembly, Mackenzie (originally from Dundee in Scotland) had become Toronto's first elected mayor in 1834. Both rebellions were given short shrift, but Lord Durham, who had arrived in Ontario on behalf of the British Government, recommended that self-government be granted and that Lower and Upper Canada be rejoined. The Province of Canada (the joining of the Lower and Upper Canada) came about through the Act of Union in 1840 and Kingston was originally chosen as the province's first capital city.

Parliamentary self-government was granted in 1848 and, by 1851, English-speaking residents far exceeded those who spoke French. The expansion of the railroad brought a further economic boom and the strength of Central Canada was further enhanced. The 1860s saw the federal union between all British North American colonies due to threats of aggression from the United States during the American Civil War combined with political stalemate between the French and English authorities. The British North America Act came into effect on July 1, 1867 and the Dominion of Canada was established with Ontario, Nova Scotia, Quebec and New Brunswick making up the four original provinces. It was also at this time that Toronto (as York had become known) became Ontario's provincial capital.

RIGHT: Shawnee chief Tecumseh (circa 1768–1813) meets his end at the hands of Colonel Richard Mentor Johnson during the Battle of the Thames, Ontario, while fighting for the British in the War of 1812 *(Getty Images 3071076 MPI/Getty Images).*

RIGHT: The Fenian Brotherhood (Irish-American) troops under the command of Colonel John O'Neill charge the retreating Queen's Own Rifles of Canada commanded by Colonel A Booker at the Battle of Ridgeway in June 1866 *(LoC pga 01485)*.

FAR LEFT: The battle, near Ridgeway Station on June 2, 1866, ended in total rout of the British troops *(LoC pga 03245)*.

LEFT: Many examples of early architecture still survive alongside the modern skyscrapers in Toronto *(Fotolia 3799056 Mary Lane)*.

LEFT: A busy canal at Sault Ste Marie at the turn of the nineteenth century *(LoC cph 3c16795)*.

ABOVE: Locals in the Rainy River District raise a barn around 1900 *(Corbis IH138761 Minnesota Historical Society/Corbis)*.

BELOW: A complete panorama of Toronto
harbor showing both the eastern and
western entrances in the early 1900s
(LoC pan 6a22572).

WESTERN DEPARTEMENTAL.   PARLIAMENTAL BUILDING.   EASTERN DEPARTEMENTAL.

Government Buildings, OTTAWA, Canada.

ABOVE: A drawing of the government buildings in Ottawa and the surrounding area in the mid-nineteenth century *(LoC cph 3b08061)*.

RIGHT: Parliament buildings in Ottawa in the 1920s *(LoC cph 3b36335)*.

RIGHT: Ottawa was first established in 1850 as "Town of Bytown" but was incorporated five years later as the "City of Ottawa" *(Getty Images 73025741 Panoramic Images).*

FAR LEFT: These rusty ore cars and locomotive in Cobalt are a reminder of the region's vast natural resources *(Getty Images 78702328 Pete Ryan).*

LEFT: The Niagara River flows over the dramatic Horseshoe Falls in Ontario meeting American Falls in New York and Rainbow Bridge in the distance *(Corbis RT003340 Charles E Rotkin/Corbis).*

RIGHT: Many have tried extraordinary feats around Niagara Falls. Here, Samuel J Dixon of Toronto walks across the Niagara River Gorge on a 7/8-inch rope above the Whirlpool Rapids on September 6, 1890. Dixon crossed from the Canadian to the American side and back again, using a balancing pole made from three fused lengths of gas pipe
(Corbis BE038329 Bettmann/Corbis).

FAR RIGHT: More than 100 years later and people are still risking their lives to cross the Falls. Jay Cochrane, 61, strolls across a cable between the Niagara Fallsview Casino and the Hilton Hotel to raise money for charity in 2005 (Corbis 42-15445403 Dick Loek/Toronto Star/ZUMA/Corbis).

The Alexandra Bridge was constructed by the Canadian Pacific Railway between 1898 and 1900 and spans the Ottawa River between Ottawa and Gatineau, Quebec *(Corbis SC001152 Paul A Souders/Corbis).*

FAR LEFT: Lightkeeper's House on Flowerpot Island in the Fathom Five National Park
(*iStockphoto 4536662 Sebastian Santa*).

LEFT: An ornate, nineteenth-century red brick house in late summer
(*iStockphoto 5523244 Gary Blakeley*).

Economics and legislation (1900–60)

Thousand Islands Bridge—constructed in 1937—crosses over the St Lawrence River between New York State and Ontario *(Getty Images 78016226 Thomas Kitchin/Victoria Hurst).*

Economics and legislation (1900–60)

One man in Ontario's development was its first Premier, the Honorable John Sandfield Macdonald (1812–72). Macdonald helped pave the way for a moderate political environment, established initially with a coalition of liberals and conservatives. He would also prove to be the last Roman Catholic Premier of the province for 132 years until 2003 when current incumbent Dalton McGuinty assumed office. However, MacDonald was defeated by liberal lawyer Oliver Mowat (1820–1903) who fought for provincial rights thereby weakening the power of the federal government. His well-argued appeals to the Judicial Committee of the Privy Council would do much to greatly decentralize Canada and give the provinces far more power than the moderate Macdonald had intended.

Further construction of the railroad through Northern Ontario and the Prairies up to British Colombia enhanced the manufacturing and industry in the province which began to flourish. During this time, minerals were beginning to play an important part in Ontario's development and mining centers to the northeast of the province at Sudbury, Cobalt and Timmins were established. The Hydro-Electric Power Commission of Ontario soon followed when it became clear that mining would need the huge resources offered by hydro-electric power. It was this cheap electric power which allowed the industry to become as important as agriculture. Two car

ABOVE: Channelled faces mark the site of lock number five on the Welland Ship Canal in August 1916. Although construction of the original canal began in 1834 it has been changed numerous times over the years and work on the current—fourth—canal began in 1913 and was completed in 1932 (LoC cph 3a44706).

RIGHT: A freighter passes through the Canal in the twenty-first century (iStockphoto 3433098 westphalia).

manufacturing plants were also formed in the early 1900s bringing new jobs and increased prosperity to the region; The Ford Motor Company of Canada (1904) and General Motors of Canada Ltd (1918). It was this last industry that would become one of the most commercially successful for the province and would provide the basis for sustained economic stability.

Like any other thriving region in a major country, Ontario underwent its fair share of changes and ideals throughout the first half of the 1900s. The Conservative government brought in Regulation 17 in July 1912 which stipulated that French-language schools would be severely limited for the province's French minority. Despite a huge outrage, Regulation 17 would remain in place until it was successfully repealed in 1927. Prohibition was brought in with the Ontario Temperance Act in 1916. Although, as already stated it was legal to distil and consume alcohol for personal consumption and producers could still export liquor for sale, it was illegal to sell alcohol (or consume it) in any other way. With prohibition a national priority in the United States, illegal alcohol was smuggled successfully from the likes of Ontario to the US. But, in 1927, the Liquor Control Board of Ontario finally brought prohibition to an end under George Howard Ferguson's (1870–1946) government.

Ontario continued to develop through the First and Second World Wars, although things were somewhat disrupted by the Great Depression (1929–33). Ontario suffered as farming, mining and logging—all essential industries in the province—were hard hit by falling prices and few, or no alternative jobs. Recovery proceeded slowly, as employment recovered quickly but productivity remained below par. The Second World War would pull Canada out of the Great Depression through an increased demand for materials in Europe. This was coupled with essential spending by the Canadian government which brought about a strong boost in the economy. And, as the economy in the United States recovered, markets for export were once again restored. Following the Second World War, Ontario was back on its provincial feet and prosperity and growth would prove exceptional.

RIGHT: The impressive façade of the Fairmont Royal York Hotel in downtown Toronto, built in 1929 (Corbis 42-16711237 Rudy Sulgan/Corbis).

RIGHT: St Sylvester's Historic Roman Catholic Church in Nipigon *(Getty Images 78711245 Pete Ryan).*

FAR RIGHT: An abandoned farmhouse on Manitoulin Island in Lake Huron *(Getty Images sb10063822o-001 Dennis McColeman).*

ABOVE: A 1948 Beechcraft floatplane on Red Lake *(Getty Images 78711386 Pete Ryan)*.

RIGHT: A Czechoslovakian worker in Batawa works on a machine gun in a factory that was originally founded to produce shoes during the Second World War *(LoC fsa 8e09274)*.

RIGHT: The Canadian War Museum in Ottawa contains thousands of exhibits that portray the country's military history. Perhaps one of the most poignant features is the Memorial Hall. Designed as a spot for rest and reflection, it contains a single artefact: the headstone of the Unknown Soldier from the First World War which is directly illuminated by the sun each Remembrance Day, November 11, at 11.00 am *(Fotolia 6119383 Gary Blakeley)*.

FAR RIGHT: Thornbury is part of the amalgamated Town of the Blue Mountains, an historic small town in rural southwestern Ontario nestled at the foot of the province's largest all-season resort, Blue Mountain *(iStockphoto 4906916 Arpad Benedek)*.

LEFT: One of the many forests that cover the Ontario landscape *(Fotolia 5266663 Paddler)*.

ABOVE: The few remaining pine trees are a stark reminder of the devastation the logging industry can wreak on the landscape *(Getty Images 77163550 Paul Damien)*.

RIGHT: Canadian timber workers sort timber that has been floated down the river in Ottawa (*Getty Images 3330022 Three Lions/Getty Images*)

FAR RIGHT: The winters can be harsh in Canada, as this picture of a tugboat and freighter at dock in a snowstorm on Lake Superior illustrates (*Getty Images ngs34_0401 Medford Taylor*).

ABOVE: A general view over Ottawa *(Fotolia 514726 Howard Sandler).*

RIGHT: Boats moored at a dock in Prince Arthur's Landing, Thunder Bay *(Getty Images 72230859 Panoramic Images).*

ABOVE: An aerial view of the sprawling Toronto suburbs *(iStockphoto 4587424 Niko Vujevic).*

RIGHT: A freight train loaded with new tractors outside the Massey Harris Company, Toronto *(Getty Images 3350491 Hulton Archive/Getty Images)*

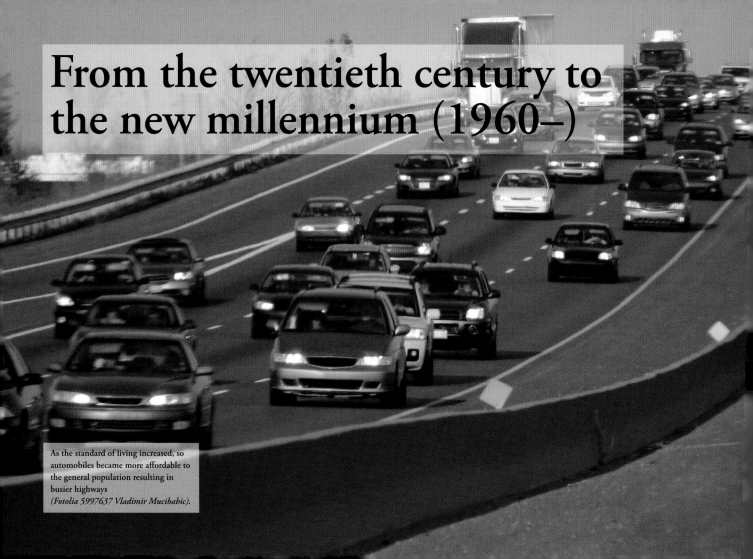

From the twentieth century to the new millennium (1960–)

As the standard of living increased, so automobiles became more affordable to the general population resulting in busier highways
(Fotolia 5997637 Vladimir Mucibabic).

From the twentieth century to the new millennium (1960–)

Ontario's rivers, including a share of the Niagara River, make the province rich in hydro-electric energy. Privatization of the industry began in 1999. However, a downturn in recent years and problems with an increase in consumption, lack of efficiency and aging nuclear reactors has meant that Ontario has had to look to its neighbors, Quebec and Michigan, to supplement its power during peak times, despite its diverse range of options. But an abundance of natural resources and excellent transportation have given the province essential links to the United States. As a result, manufacturing in Ontario has been a potent and reliable industry for the past sixty years or so. The Golden Horseshoe region is, today, the largest industrialized area nationally, and important products and exports include motor vehicles, machinery, chemicals, paper, iron, steel, electrical goods and food. Although the motor trade was initiated with General Motors and Ford—who have both seen a downturn in productivity in recent years—plans by Toyota and Honda to build manufacturing plants in the province have helped to stabilize the situation.

The center of Canada's financial services and banking industry has its home in Toronto, the province's capital, while the Information Technology sector is also based in many of its major cities. Northern Ontario is a leading region for pulp and paper manufacture while mining still plays its part here too. Central Ontario relies on a huge tourism industry which traditionally peaks during the summer months when recreational pursuits at the province's many lakes and waterways provide a relaxing atmosphere in which to enjoy the diverse wildlife. Skiing and hunting are also firm favorites with locals and tourists alike while traditional agriculture is slowly in decline with the advent of new (and some would argue, improved) technology make farming less labor-intensive. This once dominant industry now provides jobs for a much smaller percentage of the population. However, although the number of farms has steadily dropped, the actual size of farms has increased. Traditional tobacco farming has greatly decreased in favor of alternative crops while urban areas are gaining momentum which has seen the demise of productive agricultural land.

Water transportation still remains one of the most important in Ontario and the St Lawrence Seaway extends across the southern portion of the province eventually connecting with the Atlantic Ocean. It is a primary route for cargo (such as iron ore and grain). On the railroad, Ontario is connected with key cities in Canada and the United States, including Quebec and New York. The main airport in Ontario, Lester B Pearson, is the busiest in Canada and sees more than 30 million passengers through its doors each year. However, it is also an important freight and courier center. Roads, unsurprisingly, also play an important role in Ontario's

LEFT: The main street of Iroquois in the mid-1950s, before it was razed to make room for the St Lawrence Seaway and power development *(Getty Images 3334978 Central Press/Getty Images)*.

infrastructure and historically, two major east-west routes, provide essential links to neighboring provinces. Highway 401 is one of the busiest in the world. A northern route is also an important connection for cities such as Ottawa, North Bay, Sudbury and Thunder Bay. The route was first pioneered by early fur traders.

Overseen by Dalton McGuinty (born in 1955), the Premier of Ontario, the province comprises the historic towns of Ottawa, Kingston, Cornwall, Rockland, Renfrew and Perth in Eastern Ontario and Thunder Bay and the Kenora District in the north east to name but a few. The north has nine major cities which include, Timmins, Dryden and Greater Sudbury while Brampton, London, Windsor and Waterloo can all be found in the south.

With its breathtaking scenery, economic stability, diverse cultures and warm welcome, Ontario is well worth a visit.

RIGHT: Traffic at a standstill on June 15, 1959, at the junction of Bay Street and Queen Street West in Toronto during one minute of silence to remember the 81 people killed in traffic accidents in the city the previous year (*Getty Images 3329103 Fox Photos/Getty Images*)

LEFT: A 1965 view of the Parliament buildings in Ottawa, which was rebuilt after a fire in 1916 *(Getty Images 3261876 Hulton Archive/Getty Images).*

ABOVE: Cambridge was formed in 1973 when the city of Galt merged with the towns of Preston and Hespeler and parts of the townships of Waterloo and North Dumfries *(iStockphoto 4189781 Sonja Fagnan).*

LEFT: The Whirlpool Aero Car is suspended between two Canadian points over Niagara Gorge, although between these it crosses the Canadian and American borders four times on a full trip. At either end of the crossing the car is 250 feet above the river but only 150 feet in the center (*Getty Images 79382910 Henry Georgi*).

ABOVE: Crossing the suspension bridge over the River Humber at dawn in Toronto (*iStockphoto 5105691 Lorie Slater*).

Right: The town of Tobermory, at the northern tip of the Bruce Peninsula, surrounded by Lake Huron. The Bruce Peninsula lies between Georgian Bay and the main basin of Lake Huron. It extends roughly north northwestwards from the rest of Southern Ontario, pointing towards Manitoulin Island, with which it forms the widest strait, the Main Channel, joining Georgian Bay to the rest of Lake Huron (*Getty Images 73777937 Ethan Meleg*).

FAR RIGHT: While most of Canada is too cold for grape growing, Canadian wine is produced in Southern Ontario. The Niagara Peninsula is one of the largest wine producing regions and here netting is used to protect grapes from birds (*Getty Images 79382918 Henry Georgi*).

FAR LEFT: The ski slopes of Collingwood *(iStockphoto 4543836 Sebastian Santa).*

LEFT: The Museum of Civilization, designed by Douglas Cardinal, in Ottawa *(Corbis 42-19248747 Richard Bryant/Arcaid/Corbis).*

A panoramic view of Canada's
capital city, Ottawa
(iStockphoto 2064449 Tony Tremblay).

FAR LEFT: Looking along Toronto's Front East Street, with the Flatitron Building overshadowed by skyscrapers (*Getty Images 76208290 Glenn van der Knijff*).

LEFT: The United Nations Monument in Toronto against a backdrop of skyscrapers (*Getty Images 200511689-001 Grant Faint*).

ABOVE AND RIGHT: Named after Toronto's "Mayor to all the people", Nathan Phillips Square *(iStockphoto 4834882 Arpad Benedek)* is located at the foot of City Hall and is the focal point for many events throughout the year such as an ice skating rink during the winter festivities *(iStockphoto 4849736 Arpad Benedek).*

RIGHT: The Guelph Lake Dam was constructed in the 1970s to control and prevent flooding of the Speed River *(Fotolia 4581572 marcusarm).*

FAR RIGHT: A family camps on smooth, glaciated rock by the Lake of the Woods. The lake is over seventy miles long and wide, and contains over 14,552 islands *(Getty Images 78708427 Gordon Wiltsie).*

ABOVE: Ontario Place in Toronto is a highly rated attraction extending throughout three man-made islands along the Lake Ontario waterfront *(Fotolia 4525771 Gary Blakeley)*.

RIGHT: Toronto boasts a myriad of architectural styles *(iStockphoto 1836785 Elena Elisseeva)*.

LEFT: The modern face of Toronto *(Fotolia 4000503 Mary Lane)*.

ABOVE: The north face of the Royal Ontario Museum in Toronto, showing the new Michael Lee-Chin Crystal extension designed by Daniel Libeskind *(iStockphoto 5238817 Gary Blakeley)*.

ABOVE: An ice-locked boat in Collingwood Harbor with Blue Mountain in the distance *(iStockphoto 4455154 Sebastian Santa).*

RIGHT: The Trent-Severn Waterway connects Lake Ontario at Trenton with Georgian Bay at Port Severn. The Peterborough Lift Lock is pictured here *(iStockphoto 4003340 James G Charron).*

FAR LEFT: A lakeside retreat in the Muskoka countryside is one of the most desirable things for residents of Ontario. The wonderful landscape provides an escape from city life and an opportunity for recreation *(iStockphoto 4587608 Niko Vujevic)*.

LEFT: Canadian geese enjoy the sunshine on this Toronto beach *(Fotolia 848118 SamSpiro)*.

Index